INSECT WORLD

INSECT WORLD
Fly and Mosquito

Zeinab Bazyar
Roger Thomason
ITS Groups Ltd

Author Zeinab Bazyar
All photographs by Photographer Roger Thomason
All Illustration by ITS Groups Ltd
Book and Cover design by ITS Groups Ltd

Printed in the United States of America
First Printing, 2020

ISBN: 9798619333565

www.itsgroups.co.uk

Contents

INTRODUCTION

Humans are **NOT** the only creatures who are living on our planet Earth. There are other groups of animals, who are living **side** by **side** with us.

Most of the times we don't see them or understand their importance in our life until one of them **DISAPPEARS**, and then there you are.., the problems are getting started!!

The group of **insects** is one of those animals that have a very important role in our life.

There are different types of insects, in different shapes and they live in different places. Some of them are living inside the small gardens of our house, or inside of our house living with us. Some are inside the biggest forests or fields, some in deserts, or Polar Regions and so on. They can walk, fly, jump, crawl and run. Ah, do not be afraid, they are mostly **NICE**.

CHARACTERS

But wait, first, we should know what is an **insect**? How we can recognize them?

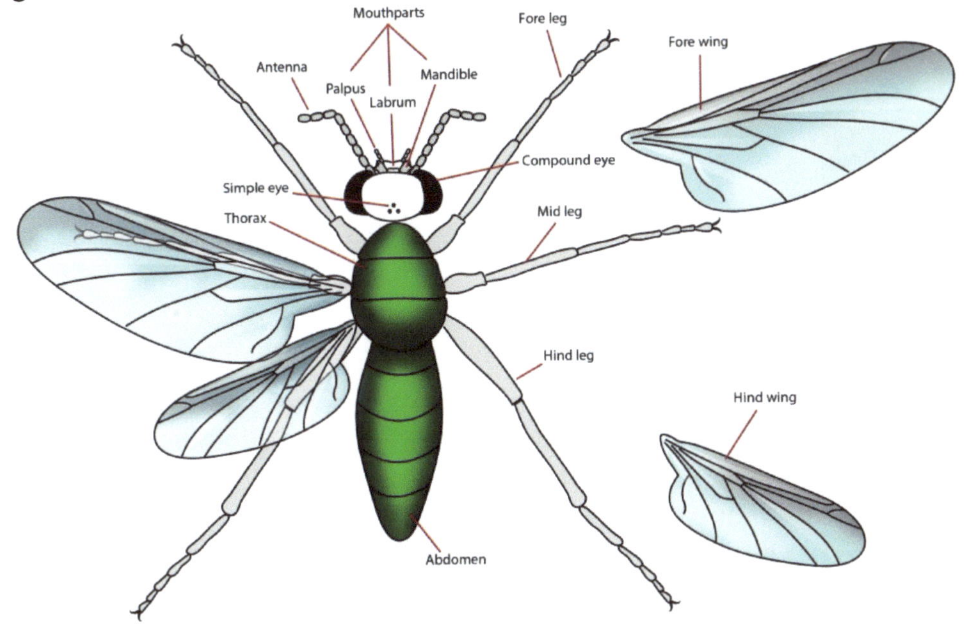

They are a group of animals who have **six** legs (**Hexapoda**), **two** antennae and their body is divided into three parts (head, chest (or thorax) and belly (or abdomen)).

They have **two** eyes like us, but their eyes are very different in shape and structures because the way they see the world is very different from us. Oh, and by the way, most of them have **three** more additional eyes too, but using them to see if there is **light** or not, and **NOT** using to see something with them.

They do not have hands but instead have **six** legs that can help them to keep their balance easily, even better than human.

The mouth of **Hexapoda** is different. It is included many structures that help them to feed themselves. These structures, **except** in three groups, are visible easily if you have a close look at them because they do not have anything to hide or cover them.

They do not have **teeth** like us, but instead, they have **jaws** up and down what helps them to chew well, but also some other parts that help them to **FEEL** the food too, or find it, or smell it!! Yes, they do not have a **nose** but some little tiny **HAIRS** and structures around their mouthparts that help them to smell and taste the food.

Just **a very few** of our six legs buddies have their mouthparts covered inside a cavity in the bottom of their head, so not so easy to see them.

Insects can have wings or **not**. If they have, it should be **FOUR** wings. The shape and function of wings can be modified in different insects. They are inserted on lateral sides of their thorax. Two of them are in the middle of thorax, called **forewings**, and the other two are on posterior part of thorax, called **hindwings**.

Some of them use all four wings to fly; some of the other use only the hindwings to fly and the forewings are protecting their hindwings, and some fly with their forewings and their hindwings **modified** to another shape to help them keep their balance and fly faster.

Insects do not have a skeleton inside of their body, but instead, they have a hardened (sclerotized) skin (Integument), which covers the entire surface of the body, and acts as a skeleton to them, and is called the Exoskeleton. It protects the body and keeps its shape. Besides that, it helps them to retain the natural fluids of the body, by stopping evaporating from the integument. The muscles, inside the body, are connected to this exoskeleton. To be able to move with this sclerotized integument, their exoskeleton is divided into small pieces. Each piece is connected to the other by a membranous area between them. That membranous area is soft and not sclerotized and so the insects from those parts can move their body.

Here there comes up a question: if the body of Hexapoda is so hard, how they can grow up then? They have to drop (molt or moult) their old exoskeleton and produce a new exoskeleton. This behaviour is called Metamorphosis.

The metamorphosis is different in hexapods. In five groups of hexapods, there is no metamorphosis. When they hatch their eggs just molting and keep continuing that several times until reaching their sexual maturity. The rest of hexapods have two different types of metamorphosis. A group has incomplete metamorphosis (Hemimetabolous) and the other group has a complete metamorphosis (Holometabolous). The difference between the holometabolous and hemimetabolous is about having an additional stage of puparium (a stage between immature and mature stages).

Egg -→ Nymph or Naiad -→ Adult   **Hemimetabolous**
Egg →larva → Pupa → Adult   **Holometabolous**
The immature stage of the holometabolous called larva, which is different in shape to their adult form. Therefore, with the stage of puparium which is the latest stage of metamorphosis they completely change their shape from larva to adult. However, in hemimetabolous insects, the immature stage named as Nymph (none aquatic) or Naiad (aquatic). They do not possess pupa (plural: pupae) and their shape is very almost similar to the shape of adults. With each metamorphosis, they get more similar to the adult shape.

The pupa also is different in shape in every group of insects. Each one has a special name, like Coarctate, Obtectate, Exarate, Cocoon.

Insects have a very huge world and their life (or **biology**) is so interesting. To learn and know more about their world we should watch them carefully, looking for them well, reading about them more, and sometimes seeing the world like them.

CLASSIFICATION

To help in our understanding of the group of animals and insects normally we **divide** them into different groups and sections. They also have a **first name** and the **last name**, like us, but with a difference of their first name is sitting **AFTER** their last name.

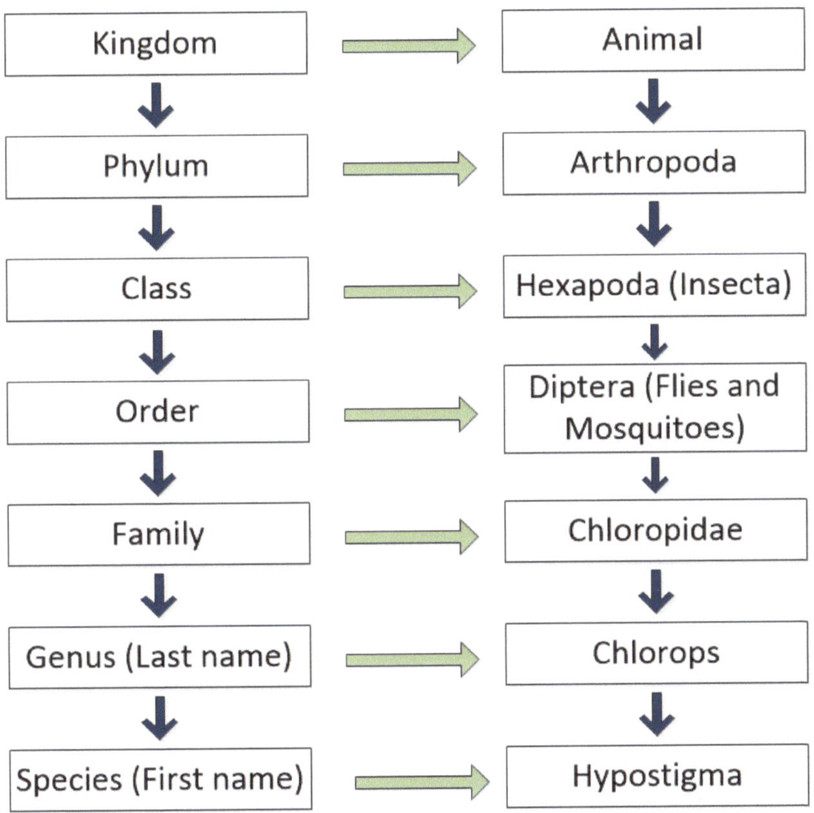

The genus and species name is specific and always and forever stays belong to that insect.

Chlorops hypostigma

Anyway, as you can see the group of insects is divided into **"ORDERS"** (included the insect groups that are similar to each other in one or more important structures. Like having **wings**, using all **four** wings or only **two**, the shape of their wings etc.).

The next group is named **"FAMILY"**. The "Families" are **inside** the "Orders". I think you know then what does it mean. Yes, it means the families are included in the groups of insects that are much similar and close to each other in shape and structures they share. Like they all have big heads, or small heads, or their wings are similar in shapes and structures on it. If you are interested like us, let's go together then and get to know with them more.

DIPTERA

In this book, we are going to know more about a group of insects, with the name of "**Flies**".

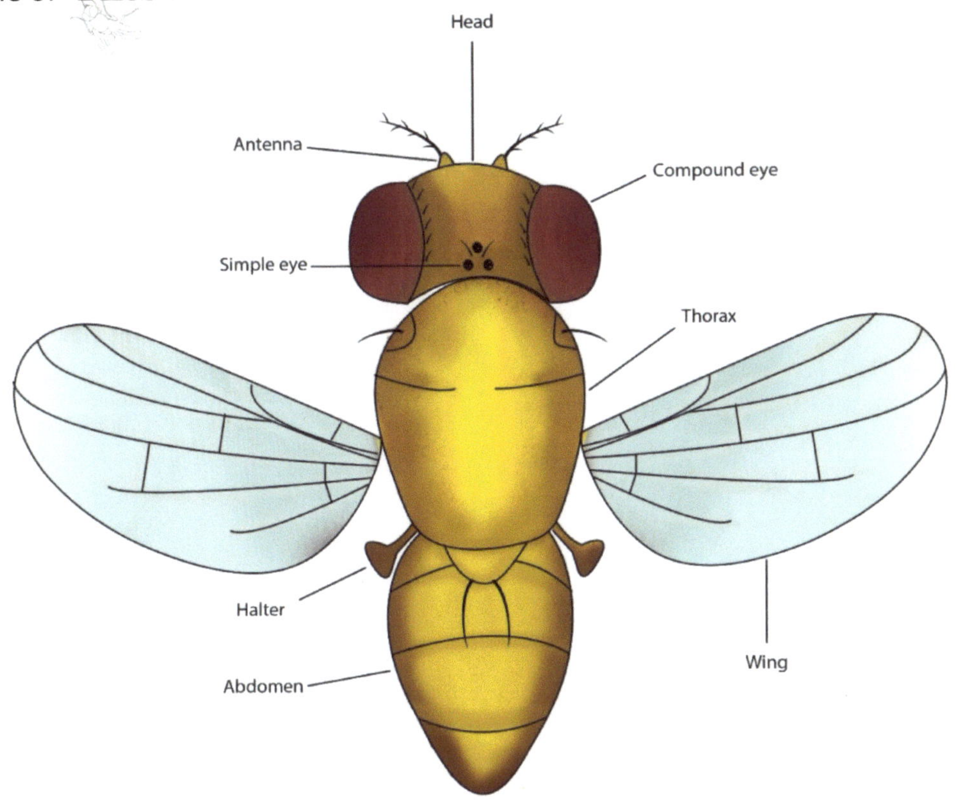

Flies (Diptera), two wings insects

This group is known as **"two-winged flies"** because they have only their forewings and their hindwings modified to a shape called a haltere. The halteres help them to keep their **BALANCE** well during flight and when they are flying fast. They will know their position in the air, as their **distance** from the ground, until the flowers or us.

The group of flies, which scientists named them "Diptera" is belonging to the holometabolous insects and divided into 2 groups: Mosquitoes and Flies.

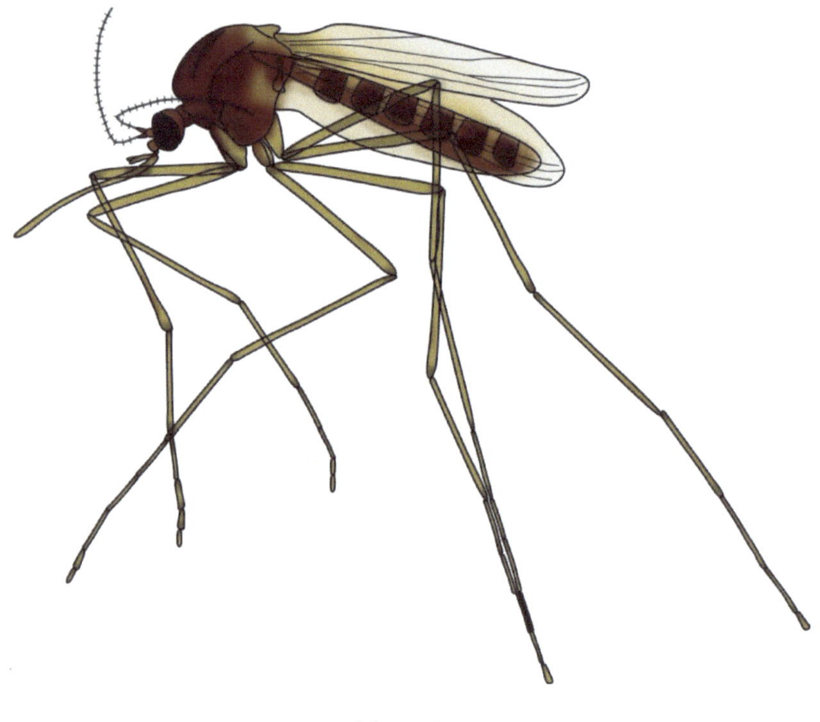

Mosquito

Mosquitoes have an elongated antenna (more than 5 segments) and most are with a very thin and elongated body. The larvae are aquatic, called "wigglers". They breathe at the surface of water upside down, through a siphon tube on 10th segment of their abdomen. They are legless and the head is well developed. Their pupa is obtectate, named commonly "tumblers".

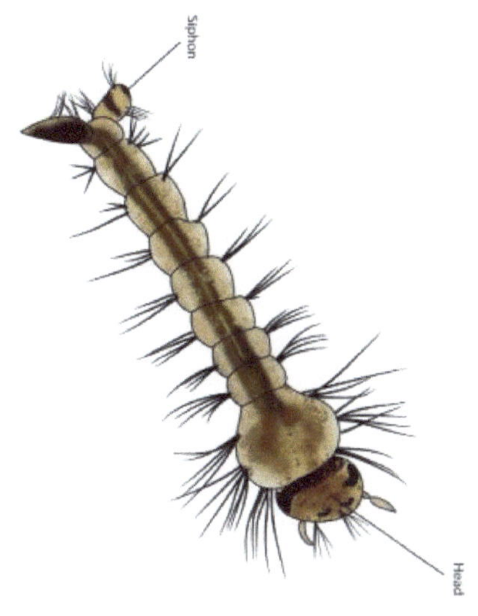

Mosquito larva

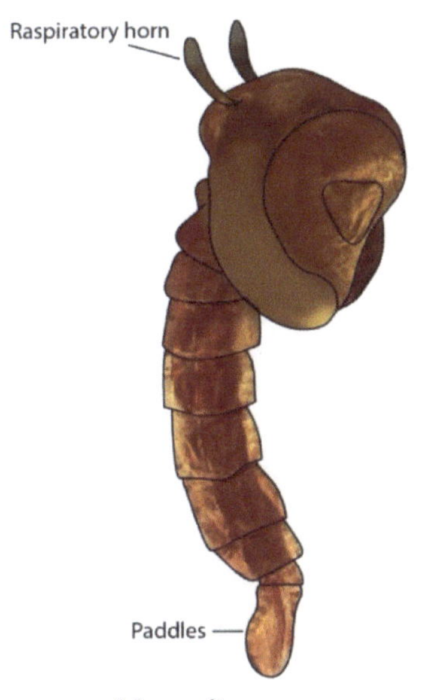

Mosquito pupa

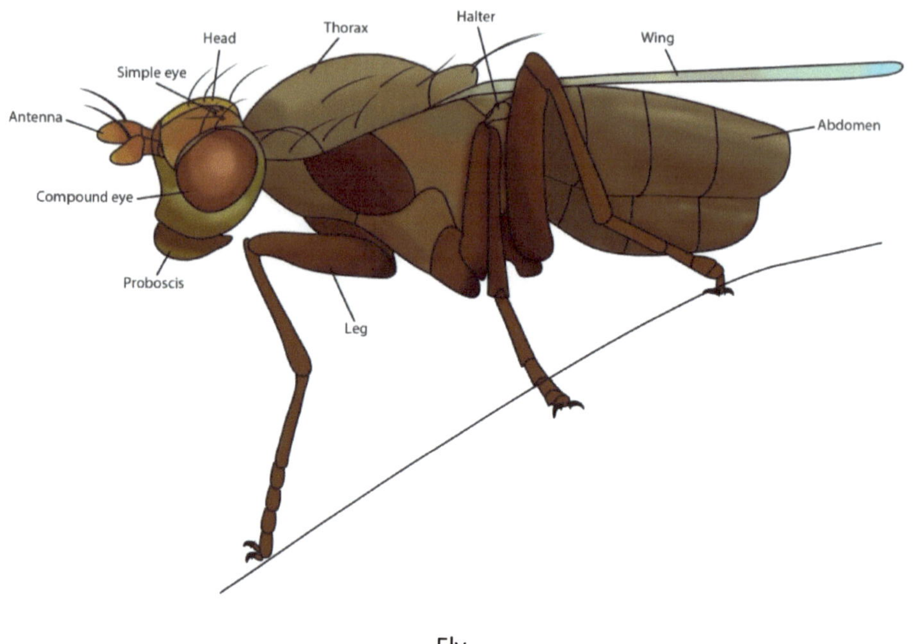

Fly

Flies have a very short antenna (less than **5** segments) and their bodies are not narrow but more or less rounded or **oval**. The larvae are less aquatic than the mosquitos, called "maggots". They are legless and the head is not developed and strongly reduced. The pupa is coarctate.

Fly larva

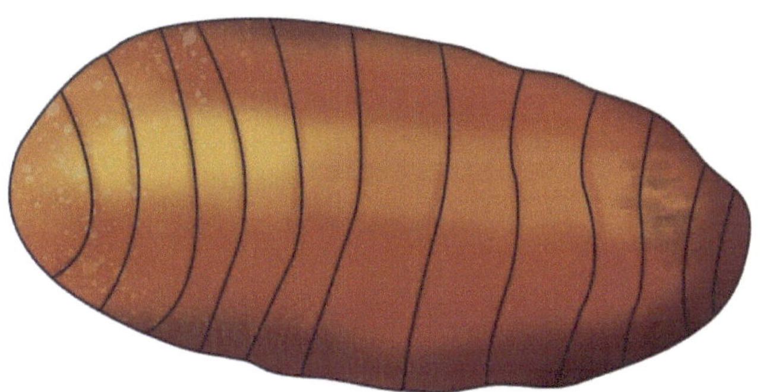

Fly pupa

In the following pages, you can find different shapes and species of flies and mosquitoes, and some basic information about their biology, as where you can find them and what they are eating.

Zeinab Bazyar

Mosquitoes

Name: ANISOPODIDAE (wood gnats or window gnats)

Larvae feed on wet, decaying or fermenting organic matter like dead plants or animals.

Adults feed on the nectar of **FLOWERS**.

Name: BIBIONIDAE (march flies, love-bugs)

Figure 1: Male ♂

Figure 2: Female ♀

Larvae live in the top layers of soil and leaf litter. They are important in helping to form and shape the soil. They feed on leaf litter, decaying organic material, and sometimes in rotten wood and dung.

Adults are having a short life of between three to seven days. They can be seen on flowers, feeding on nectar or **pollen**, and sometimes **honeydew**.

Name: CECIDOMYIIDAE (gall midges)

Larvae are found on **fungi** and decaying plant material. They can be on all parts of living plants, and among other groups of insects. Some of them are predators of other insects. Some of the adults are plant-feeders that can live only one or two days, but the adults that are feeding on fungus and predators can live longer. The adults that take nectar have among them some groups who are important **pollinators**.

Name: CHAOBORIDAE (phantom midges)

The larvae are often restricted in standing **WATER**, from small pools to large lakes. They have a **TRANSPARENT** body and are predaceous. These larvae wait for prey when they are passing nearby they detect them with their sensory hairs. The larvae capture the prey and eat them.

The larvae do not have gills, so to stay underwater they need to bring with themselves oxygen underwater. They control the oxygen by making a bubble (air sac) by raising to the surface of water frequently. They do this activity during the late evening, and during daylight, they go to deeper water and consume the collected oxygen until night.

The adults get **attracted** to the nearby lights.

Name: CHIRONOMIDAE (non-biting midges)

Some of the larvae are predators of other groups of **invertebrates** (those that do not have **SPINES** in their body) or parasites of other animals like fish. A few of them are miners inside of some plant's leaves.

The adults live short lives on the wing, between hours to a few weeks. They feed on the nectar of flowers or honeydew. They never bite.

Name: CULICIDAE (mosquitos, zancudos)

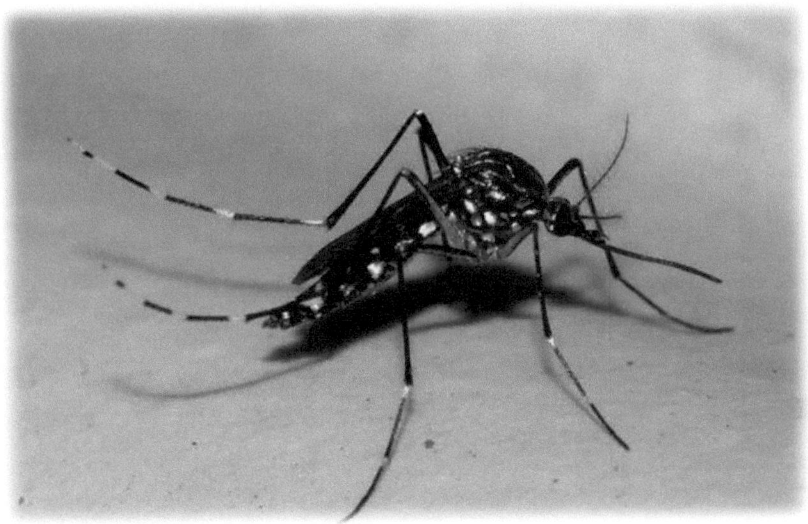

Larvae develop in **wet** habitats, like pools, lakes, the holes in rocks or trees and water contained in fallen fruit, and artificial containers. They feed on floating organic material like pollen grains, the particle material has fallen into the water; and some are predaceous.

Adults generally are feeding on nectar and pollen. Some others feed on honeydew, fruit juices, and sap secreted from the stems and leaves of plants.

Name: LIMONIIDAE (crane flies 1)

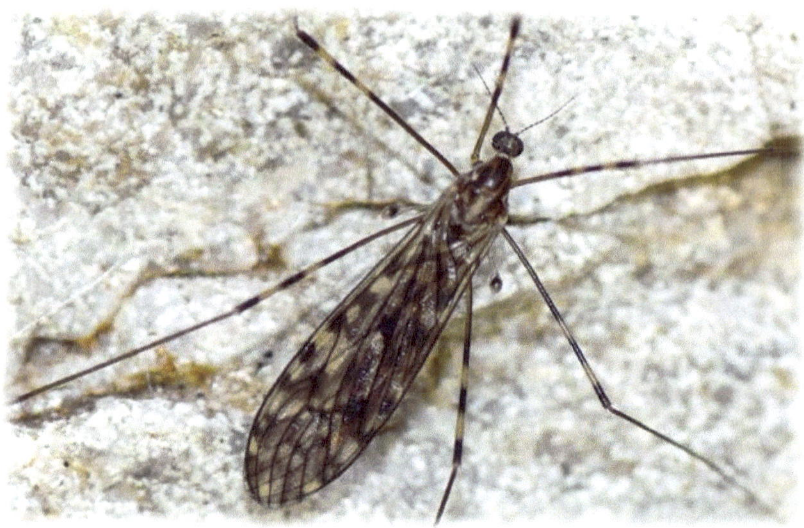

Larvae are aquatic or semi-aquatic (half-aquatic). So, they depend on freshwater, including flowing waters or standing waters on algae, moss and rocks. Also, they are seen on **decaying** wood and rotting plants.

Adults are active around open waters, shaded areas in forests, cultivated areas, grasslands and urban areas.

Name: PSYCHODIDAE (sand flies, and moth flies or owl flies)

Larvae are mostly terrestrial found in soil, usually in semi-desert (half-desert) areas. Some of them are living in soil and rotting wood. Some are living in moist or semi-aquatic areas. Some groups inside this family have **MEDICAL** importance. The adults feed on the blood of humans and animals and can transfer diseases. They are flies that are often found in bathrooms and toilets which have earned them the name of Drain-flies.

Name: TIPULIDAE (crane flies 2)

This group can usually be found in humid environments like the margins of ponds and streams, but some of them are found in forests, cultivated fields and urban yards.

Sweepings or other types of traps can capture adults easily. They are resting mostly on vegetation, where is close to the place that reproduces their larvae.

The adults mostly have a vestigial mouthpart and therefore a very short life because they cannot feed themselves, although, some species have a complete mouthpart and taking the nectar of flowers.

This family is important to us as some of the larvae can help to process the dead organic materials, like dead plants.

25

Flies

Name: AGROMYZIDAE (leaf-mining flies)

Larvae of all species feed on living plant tissues. They live in different places such as roots, stems, seeds, flower head, trunk, twigs and sometimes are like leaf **miners**.

Adults feed sometimes on the sap of plants, where they lay their eggs.

Name: ANTHOMYIIDAE (anthomyiid flies)

The adults are visitors to plants and have an important role in pollination. They feed on **NECTAR** and pollen. Some species are feeding on honeydew or the sap secreted from wounded trees and fruit. Some are feeding on dung and carrion too.

The larvae are scavengers, herbivores (feeding on herbs) and fungivores (feeding on fungus).

Name: ASILIDAE (robber flies, assassin flies)

All of them are predators. They feed on other insects, or sometimes on other groups of animals, like spiders.

Larvae are predators or parasites too, but there is very little information about their **biology**. The larvae can live about four to seven years until they turn into an adult.

Name: BOMBYLIIDAE (bee flies)

Adults are often resting and sunning themselves on trails, rocks, or twigs. They feed on flowering plants because they are nectar feeders and the females are pollen feeders. Because of this, the bee flies are one of the big groups of pollinators on different flowering plants. Some of the plants are dependent on this group to pollinate.

Larvae are predators or parasitoids of other groups of insects or other groups of **ARTHROPODS** (a huge group including the group of insects whose bodies are segmented).

Name: CALLIPHORIDAE (blowflies)

Adults feed on all forms of carrion and faeces as well as on honeydew and nectar. Some of them are important pollinators of mango and in mango orchards. When these trees are in **bloom**, we can find many of these flies around them.

Some of the species are also important in forensic and police investigations.

Name: CARNIDAE (carnid flies)

Larvae are found feeding on decaying organic material.

Adults can be found close to **bird**'s nests and mammal animal's burrows, or on decaying vegetation and dung.

Name: CHAMAEMYIIDAE (chamaemyiid flies)

32

Larvae are all predators of other insects, like bugs and wasps.
There is little information about adults. But, some groups of adults scratch the backs of bugs and feed on their honeydew secretions from their body.

Name: **CHLOROPIDAE (frit flies, grass flies, eye gnats)**

They have many different types of lifestyles. The larvae are feeding on plants or decaying material. Some of them are a predator of other groups of insects or arthropods. Some are a parasite of other animals like **frogs**.

The adults are pollinators of plants; some of them feed on stored foods of other arthropods (kleptoparasite). There is limited information about the biology of the members of this group.

Some species of this family can transmit diseases to humans and animals.

Name: COELOPIDAE (kelp flies)

All larvae are found living close to the sea on beaches. They live in seaweed and especially kelp.

Adults sometimes move together in swarms which can be annoying for the people using the beach.

Name: CONOPIDAE (thick-headed flies)

The adults are mostly endoparasites of bees and wasps, grasshoppers, specifically of cockroaches and crickets. They can be found on flowers.

The larvae develop **INSIDE** the body of other insects and feeding on them. In the end, the larvae attack the body tissue of insects and kill them to get out their body.

Name: **DIASTATIDAE (diastatid flies)**

There is no information about the biology of larvae.
The adults are flying around low shrubs and along the margins of marshes.

Name: DOLICHOPODIDAE (long-legged flies)

Adults are often found running on leaves, tree trunks, mud and river rocks. They are still very good fliers and predators on soft-bodied animals like mites and insects. Because of this, they have some importance in **pest** control in agriculture.

The larvae are living in soil, rotted vegetation, mud, under bark and holes of trees. They are predators or feeding on decaying material.

Name: DROSOPHILIDAE (small fruit flies, pomace flies, vinegar flies)

There are so many lifestyles in this group, but they are mostly known for breeding on decaying fruits and vegetables.

There are a very famous species in this family that is always used in experimental research called Drosophila melanogaster (last name and first name of that species).

The larvae feed on the yeasts and bacteria in rotting fruits, and the adults are breeding in rain forests. Still, some other species are living on flowers, fresh fungi, the sap of the trees, leaf-mining, and some of the others are living like a predator or parasite of other groups of insects or animal, like frog's eggs.

If your **TRASH** is not emptied on time, this group of flies will quickly multiply there and spread around the house.

Name: DRYOMYZIDAE

The larvae can be found in decaying organic materials, decaying fungi and dung. Some of them are predators of barnacles.

There is **NO** information yet about the adult's biology.

Name: EMPIDIDAE (dance flies, balloon flies, predaceous flies)

Larvae are commonly found in moist soil, dung, rotten wood, or in humid areas. Sometimes they are predaceous on many other groups of insects especially other flies larvae.

Some of the adults in this family are predaceous and preying the other groups of insects, some of the others are flower-visitors and feeding on pollen and a few taking nectars. They are found in forests, on the leaves, tree trunks, or aquatic vegetation.

Some of the adults in flight look like they are **dancing** in the air, and because of this, they are called **dance flies**.

Name: EPHYDRIDAE (shore flies)

The members of this family are aquatic and semi-aquatic. They are active around muddy and freshwater areas.

Larvae feed on **MICROORGANISMS** like bacteria, unicellular algae and yeasts, by filtering them. A few of them like to feed on decaying material or excrement.

Adults mostly feed on microscopic algae.

Name: FANNIIDAE (fanniid flies, laterine flies)

Larvae are feeding on decaying organic matter, including rotting plant material, latrines, dung, and carrion.

Adult **males** are seen hovering around together as **females** are sitting on the vegetation watching them. A few species are known to be attracted to sweat and body secretions.

Name: HELEOMYZIDAE (heleomyzid flies)

43

Many of these flies are living in places that have shadows. Areas like cool forests. But, some of them also are living in dry and sandy areas. Some species are living in **bird** nests, **rodent** burrows, and some living close to **bats**.

Name: LAUXANIIDAE (lauxaniid flies)

Larvae feed on decaying plant material, associated with fungi, **bacteria** and yeasts.

Adults feed on leaves with their specially modified mouthparts that are useful for grazing.

Name: LONCHAEIDAE (lance flies)

Most of the known larvae are scavengers, breeding especially in damaged plants or decaying vegetation. Some are attacking living plants.

The adults are mostly living close to other groups of insects, like under bark of trees with some beetles that are living there too, or close to some groups of mosquitoes. Some species also get attracted to damaged fruits or plants.

Name: **LONCHOPTERIDAE (spear-winged flies)**

Larvae are feeding on decaying vegetation.
Adults are found in many habitats, feed on fungi, nectar, pollen, and dead insects.

Name: MICROPEZIDAE (stilt-legged flies)

47

This group is mostly seen walking on leaves or similar places, close to ants and wasps and **mimicking** the movement and shape of them.

Larvae feed on dung and decaying vegetables. Several species feed on decaying wood too.

Adults get attracted to dung.

Name: MUSCIDAE (houseflies, stable flies)

This family can be found almost everywhere.

Their larvae living in habitats like dung, **garbage**, fungi, fresh or decomposing fruit and vegetable, etc., and feeding on other insects, faeces, decaying material, rarely on plants. A few species feed on bird's blood.

The adults have also different types of biology. Some of them are predators of other insects, some feeding on pollen and acting as a pollinator, others consume the decaying material which is so important, and some of them feeding on the blood of animals and sometimes even **humans**.

Name: **OPOMYZIDAE (cereal flies)**

The larval mainly feed on cereals and legumes. Some of them are feeding inside the stem of plants.

Adults are active in open areas.

Name: PALLOPTERIDAE (flutter flies)

Larvae are found living under the bark of dead coniferous and deciduous trees. They are a predator of the groups of beetles who are living there too.

The adults rest on the low branches and flowers; sometimes attracted to the LIGHT.

Name: PHAEOMYIIDAE

There is no information yet about members of this family. There is just a few on one species of the group whose larva is a parasitoid of millipedes.

Name: PHORIDAE (hump-backed flies, scuttle flies)

Larvae are scavengers, feeding on plants, predators of other insects, stealing food from other food stores of other insects, parasitoids, and parasites of other insects.

Adults feed mostly on the honeydew of leaves, on nectar, spores of fungus and pollen. Some of them are predators of other insects or attacking other insects to lay their eggs on their bodies.

Name: PIOPHILIDAE (skipper flies)

Larvae are scavengers, breeding mainly in protein-rich plant and animal material. They can be found in bird nests, sometimes can breed in fungi or rotting wood. Some of the larvae in this group can **jump** or **skip** which is a special character for this family and could not be seen in the other groups of flies.

About the biology of adults, there is not yet any information.

Name: PIPUNCULIDAE (big-headed flies)

Larvae live inside the body of the other immature or adult insects.

Adults are frequently seen hovering among vegetation, and their flight is similar to that of Syrphidae (that you will read about later). They can be seen in open areas of forest and along forest edges.

The Adults feed on honeydew and sometimes on secretions of other insects. If you want to attract them, just make a mixture of honey, **Coca-Cola** and water and spray on a small part of the vegetation.

Name: **PSILIDAE (rust flies, psilid flies)**

Larvae are feeding on trees or herbaceous plants. They can live in the burrow made in pine trees or under the bark of trees infested by a group of beetles.

There is no information about the biology of the adults.

Name: RHAGIONIDAE (snipe flies)

Larvae are probably aquatic and living close to stream-side vegetation, or maybe found in MOIST soil that is rich in organic material. They are predators of other groups of insects.

Adults are maybe predators too, but still, there are some doubts about that and needs more study to confirm this **behaviour**.

Name: RHINIIDAE (nose flies)

There are some **MEDICALLY** important issues about the members of this group. Some of the larvae are active in the eggs of **other** insects or inside the nest of termites. There is no information yet about the larvae and adults of this family.

Name: RHINOPHORIDAE (woodlouse flies)

58

Larvae are parasitoids of some insects like **termites**.
No information about adults.

Name: SARCOPHAGIDAE (flesh flies)

Some of the larvae are feeding on dead animals and some others are parasitoids/predators on other insects, snails and **reptiles**. A species in this group is feeding on stored foods of some species of wasps. As read earlier, this behaviour is called "kleptoparasitism".

Most of the adults are **sun-loving** and can find them in small sunspots on the ground inside the humid areas like forests and river beaches.

Name: SCIOMYZIDAE (snail-killing flies, marsh flies)

Larval feeding habits are complex and varied inside the family; most are primary parasitoids or predators on freshwater or terrestrial molluscs and are predaceous on aquatic or terrestrial snails, slugs, and a few on fingernail clams.

There is not enough information about the adults' feeding and **behaviour**, but they have activity in vegetation.

Name: SEPSIDAE (black scavenger flies)

The larvae are mostly feeding on mammalian faeces, but also sometimes on decaying organic materials.

The adults are gathering around cowpats and sometimes around faeces of wild mammals. They are resting normally on low herbs.

Name: SPHAEROCERIDAE (small dung flies)

The larvae are microbial **CONSUMERS**. They are active in a humid area that is full of bacteria. They can be found in dung, carrion, and different types of decomposing vegetation and fungi.

Adults also can be found on microhabitats and decaying vegetation like tree falls.

Name: **STRATIOMYIDAE (soldier flies)**

They can be found mostly in decaying plant material like leaf litter to rotting fruit. Found under the bark of fallen trees too.

Larvae are aquatic, found in a variety of wet habitats like ponds and rivers.

Adults are often found sitting on the leaves in **sunny** patches in the forest habitats and some adults visit flowers.

Name: SYRPHIDAE (flower flies)

The larvae have a wide variation in their biology. Some of them feed on decaying material of coffee and wasted material of orange juice. Some are predators and have agricultural importance in controlling pests like Aphids (greenfly).

The adults are mostly very similar to **bees** and wasps in colour. Most of them are found on FLOWERS, and some of the others are pollinators. They can fly in one place (hovering), like a helicopter.

Name: TACHINIDAE (tachinid flies, parasitic flies)

Larvae are parasitoids of other groups of insects. They grow inside the body of other insects and then as they are growing finally they kill their host and get out of its body.

The adults try to find a host to lay their eggs on the body of the prey, so their larva can enter inside the body of the host to feed. This group has importance in agricultural biological control because they can be used to **control** the pests found on crops.

Name: TEPHRITIDAE (fruit flies)

They are mostly feeding on different plant tissues, like fruits, seeds, flowers, leaves, stems, or roots. But, also there is a species that is a parasitoid of a group of insects, among the butterflies.

The adults usually feed only on liquid material like HONEYDEW, bird faeces and plant secretion.

Name: ULIDIIDAE (picture -winged flies)

There isn't much information about the biology of this group. Larvae of most of the group are feeding on decaying materials. Some of them are living under the bark of some types of trees like pines, poplars, aspens etc. some others maybe live on some other type of plants that already have been attacked by other insects like **corns, bananas, tomatoes, cherries, coconuts**, etc.

Adults are often attracted to decaying materials and composts.

References

Brake, I. 2011. The new Diptera site, Phaeomyiidae. Access from

http://diptera.myspecies.info/content/phaeomyiidae-0

Brown, B.V., Borkent, A., Cumming, J.M., Wood, D.M., Woodley, N.E. & Zumbado, M.A., Manual of Central American Diptera. *National Research Council of Canada*, Ottawa.

De Jong, Y. et al. 2014. Fauna Europaea. Access from www.Fauna-eu.org

Falk, S. 2011. Flicker, Rhiniidae (nose flies). Access from https://www.flickr.com/photos/63075200@N07/collections/7215770 1366469304/

Kirk-Spriggs A.H. and Sinclair B.J., Manual of Afrotropical Diptera. Suricata 4. Pretoria: South African National Biodiversity Institute.

Mc.Alpine, J.F., Peterson, B.V., Shewell, G.E., Teskey, H.J., Vockeroth, J.R. and Wood, D.M. Manual of Nearctic Diptera. Biosystematics Research Centre (formerly Institute) Ottawa, Ontario.

Papp, L. & Darvas, B., Contributions to A Manual of Palaearctic Diptera (with special reference to flies of economic importance). Science Herald Press, Budapest.